painting the inside

painting the inside

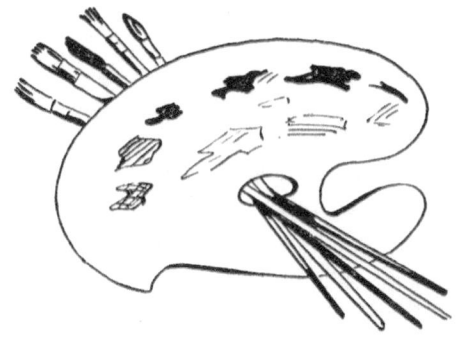

t.w. bilheimer

Library of Congress Control Number:		2011919197
ISBN:	Softcover	978-1-4653-8713-4
	Ebook	978-1-4653-8714-1

To order additional copies of this book, contact:
Xlibris Corporation
1-888-795-4274
www.Xlibris.com
Orders@Xlibris.com

to the singer-
who challenged my edges
and-
inspired my words.

painting the inside

feeling to thought-
thought to heart-
heart to hand-
and-
hand to words
cast downward
in
splatter shape-
paintings
of inside
take form
and life-
to dwell within
the reader's
eye.

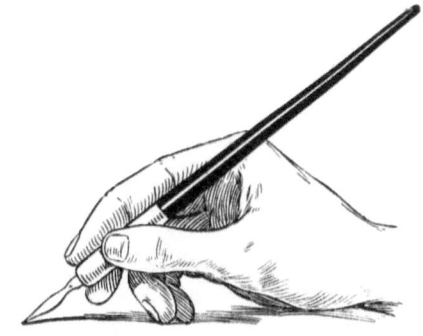

words they fly

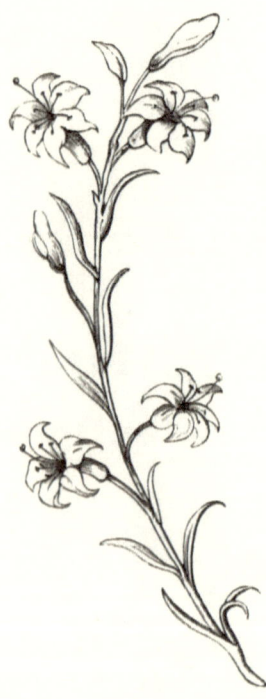

words they fly
from poets mind-
droplets in a pitcher
of thought-
cast downward
to page,
water to ground,
on mid-winters wings.

frozen words
like ice
shimmering,
black,
in the eye
of readers'
stare.

wicked and stealthy

wicked and stealthy
the ways of women-
teasing the soul,
twisting the mind,
slanting all thought
till-
nothing adds,
nothing fills
sensible sum-
and
crooked ways
seem real-
in the
fantasy that
once was
love.

they dwell together

they dwell together
these children of life,
yes-
and no-
under one roof
in combat joined.

for yes
tells risk-
as the fledgling
falls from
safest nest
to the glory
of freedom flight.

no gives comfort-
for in her
embrace
no broken bones
prevail-
and the nest
extends
embracing arms
tho gray
they may be.

equally then they-
children
of parent fear-
wrestle on lifes' fringes.

one coin
of divergent
face-
awaiting
the truth
of
their fate.

B

white spaces

mystery
bubbles upward
from white spaces
'tween words-
gushing vulcan fire,
or
childs soft sigh-
upward they spew
from sacred
realms-
then
freeze to page
like
so much spilt water
on
winter's
chill ground.
for -
in these white
spaces-
these zephers
of mind
dwell
all of all
that is,
or can
be.

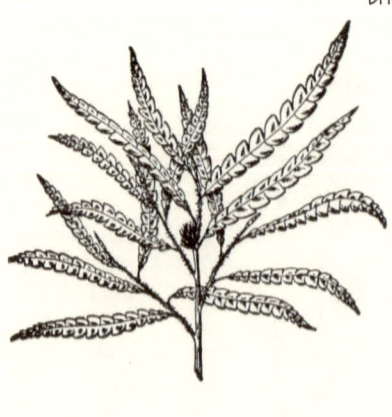

velvet

velvet this summer eve's landscape-
hard upon a well earned solstice,
wrapped loosely
in quick'ning
twilight
peeking through
trees-
and falling
'pon
spring's gift'd ground
of greenery
so lush.

touch these gifts
lightly
and savor-
yet hold them
with an artist's caress-
for they are as fleeting
as the junebug-
whose sudden rise-
graces
this dusk burnished
moment.

the same moon

&

we see the same moon,
you and me-
casting shadows
of
pearly light-
'or
pennsylvania hills-
and
new york
trees.

we see the same moon,
you and me-
layering lace
of
pure white-
'or
frozen field
and
crystalline
pond.

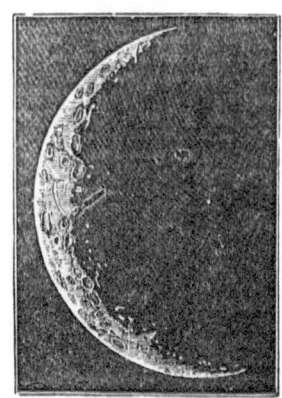

we see the same moon,
you and me-
with creative eye
that
frames all light-
and
gently paints
our
inner
glow.

we see that same moon,
you and me.

unattainable that star

unattainable that star
just a breath away-
yet distant
as
venus.

beautiful and mysterious
her
presence quickens-
making love-thought
long sleeping
leap to life
in color'd shade
to become whole-
in the
depths
of
a sleeping soul.

truth came visiting then

truth came visiting then-
a vagrant
in a callous land
of
hard souls
grabbing,
tearing,
ripping,
that which was-
till
only tortured scraps
remained-
in the shadow
of
truth
revealed.

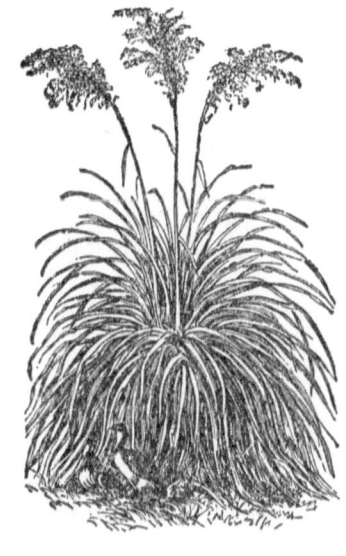

this void

this void
this loss
of all-
stretching behind
and before-
a yawning hole in the fabric
of being.

yet
that which is empty
will be full-
for nature abhors
the vacuum
of space-
without
meaning.

and so-
as leaves fall
to
full growth in spring-
so shall
the void be full-
...in His time.

thanksgiving

this day
of
family
and
friends
brimm'd full-
laughter
and warmth
set apart
from daily drudge-
soothes
soul
and heart-
rounding
square'd edges-
to
smiles
of thanks-
for
the joy
of
life.

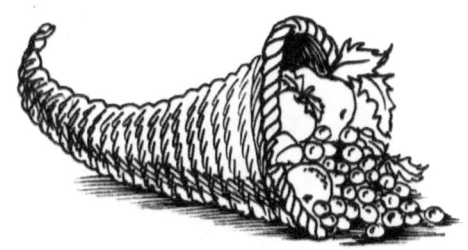

the songstress

the wordsmith saw beauty
that beaconed afternoon,
'mongst glass blown splendor-
a flower of
lovliness reserved
for rare few.

the wordsmith saw prettiness
one velvet eve,
near sailboats' stout mast-
a smile reflected
in sunset's
deep glow.

the wordsmith saw splendor
on a bone white beach,
'neath gulls with full wing-
an image of delicacy
framed by
soft gentle waves.

the wordsmith saw shapeliness
under noonday sun
midst sunken blooms-
an elegant rose
smiling -'midst
lesser petals.

God's artistry was seen
by the wordsmith's senses,
down the corridors of dream-
an image of beauty
rare as gold
in the purple haze of night.

...the wordsmith saw
the songstress-
and smiled in
wonder.

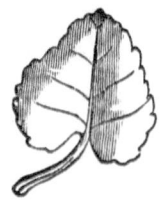

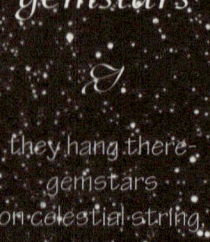

gemstars

they hang there–
gemstars
on celestial string,
icy
cold
twinkles of eternity,
holding eye fast
in stilled silence
down corridors
of
timeless time,
round the corners of
soul.

the wheel it turns

the it wheel turns
as always will-
light to dark
and in reverse-
shades of gray
to sparkling white
in following wake-
past mountains
of joy
or hurt-
near rivers
of tears
or laughter-
to find new
life
in
the streaming sunrise-
new,
curious shape-
in
the soft
gathering
dawn.

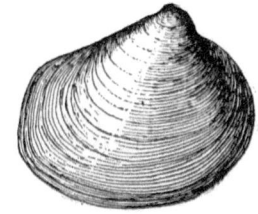

the mother

ᔥ

the mother
could see...

in life's knowing ways-
her smile
that shown
like a beacon to shore
in a mariners night-
her choice-
the
tilt of
her heart-
'neath
air filled
rush-
of
white layer'd dreams...

the mother could see...

ℬ

a quiet valley

the cycle of
seasons
or-
rhythm of
growth and harvest-

the falling of feather-like
snow
or-
shimmering of
ice 'pon crystalline pond-

the pitched squeal of
childrens' laughs
or-
crink'ld grin of
season'd folk-

spell
time without time-
in
our peaceful valley.

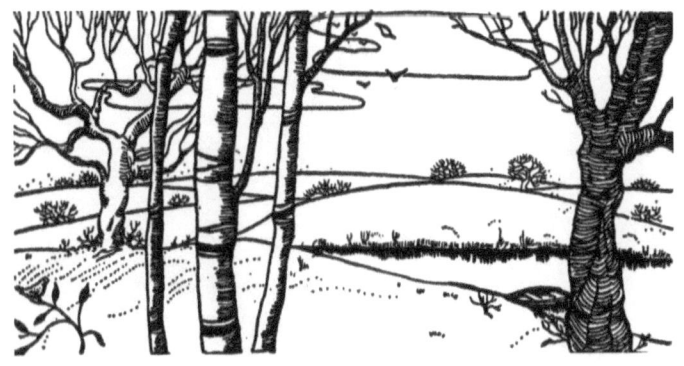

the colors of love

the colors of love
eyed through
the prism of caring,
split to myriad hue-

soft and gentle
as morn's purple dew-
fire red
as the noonday sun-
light dancing gray
as afternoons' cool shadows-
or murmured orange
of a deep summer sunset.

each shade spells
mystery-
each muted tone
or shouted burst-
a painted thread
in kaleidoscope
symphony,
heard only by those-
whose eyes
over years,
saw its color
unfold-
in sudden
blinding wonder.

that snow

that snow
now hard
with icy crust-
shimmering
slipmaking
to unwary
foot or paw-
lying
in wait
for
misstep
taken-
as the tiger
in lair-
muscled to
spring
upon thoughtless
prey.

summer rain

summer rain
tapping gently
on skylight high-
sends a message of
cool cleansing
midst seasons's
heat-
gently telling
all who will hear
a nature-code message
of pause
and
reflection-
in the mysterious
quiet corners,
of a
dark
and velvet spun
june
eve.

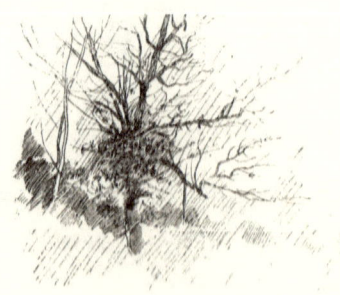

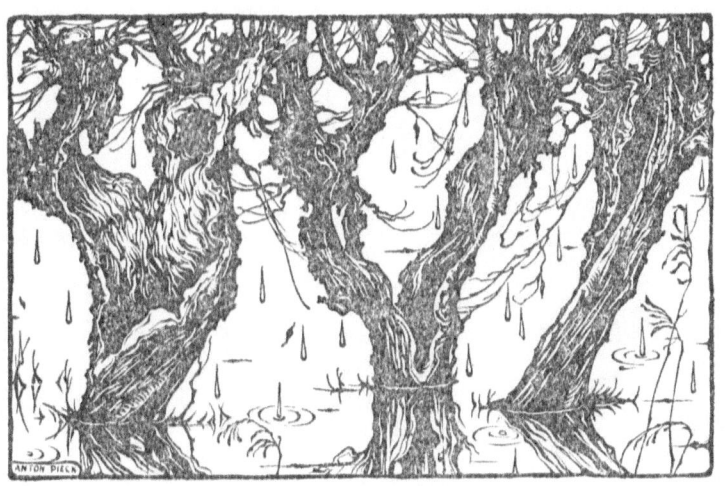

such a rain

such a rain on my roof
of tin-
tapping out the day
under leaden sky-
rhythm of nature
in
staccato counterpoint-
nourishing the earth
and
me-
...to yet greater vista.

chaos of ice

midst
the chaos of ice,
near falling water's edge
shines
a new mint'd
star,
fated to be
gone with
the morrows sun-
living its life
of
diamond cut
splendor-
in faceted glory
no man
can
fashion.

'tis the
work
of Hands
with mysterious digit-
crad'ling
the palette-
of star ice
and men.

frozen specks

shredded- frozen specks
they fall-
white,
crystalline,
and pure.

worlds within worlds
they blanket-
feathery
bumps
on crystal waters...
soon to
dissolve
and flow-
to eternal
sea.

flakes and people-
you and me-
different
yet same-
riders
on winds
of
drifted snow-
near the edges
of timeless
white mystery.

slanted shadows

slanted shadows
of afternoon
glare-
cast shadows
of changing shape
o'r mysterious
white plains
of frozen beauty-
telling
all who care
to glimpse their hue-
of mysteries
beyond
mere ice shaded
gray.

for-
in this
dancing,
sun born light-
lives
truths
only heard-
by
stillness filled
ears-
listening
with
quiet eye'd
glance
toward the borders
of
thought.

_B_

beaconed afternoon

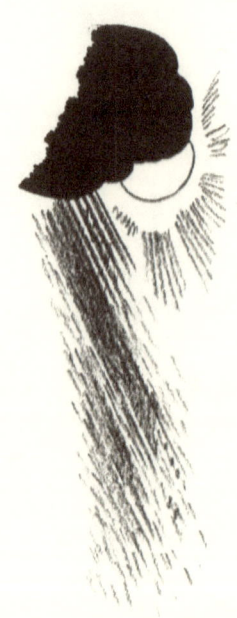

how odd
this turn of two
so long apart-
friendship
near galleried space
'mongst mountains
and song-
sharing sunshine
words-
and thought.

so long
a gestation
this-
as the pearl grows
from sand grain
small...
slowly-
to
brilliant
fate.

needl'd fingers

rain downward drilling
like bullets
to earth in frantic
rhythm-
scouring earthbound
things
with needl'd fingers-
of icy
life.

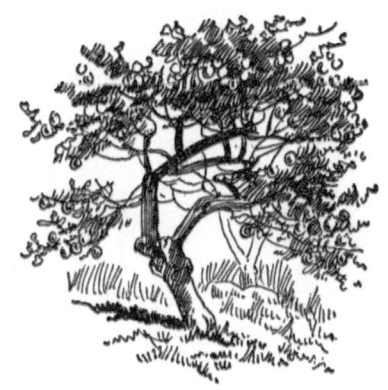

ice's season

&

ice's season
of rock hard crystal
and frozen pond-
entombs all landscape
in durable grip.
diamond faceted
mansions
of bold ego'd
permanence-
birth whispers
of forever
with blank stare belief.
still...
secretly...
even stealthily,
pin rays
of the star
slice april colored lines

in illusion-
giving lie to forevers.
for-
as colors sprout
on yielding ground-
gaudy markers sagely
tell-
in tender shoots-
neither ice
nor
steel-
nor stark rigid souls-
hold permanent
tread
'pon the eternal flux-
Life.

have you seen a day?

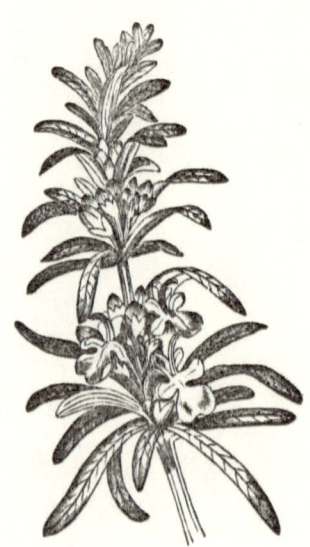

have you seen a day
clear of sky
with fast racing clouds
dancing-
on a
floor of blue?

have you seen a day
fresh in newness-
with bracing breeze
whistling thru
forested branch?

a day of
power-
of hope-
of energy-
untapped.

take this day
outward to
in-
and fly
toward all dreams'
core-
in fullness wrought
on the wind
of passion.

on gray-tinge'd days

on gray-tinge'd days
of mist fill'd air
and
leaden sky-
of puddl'd wood
and
swollen stream-
of
mid march drear
and
sepia lines-

on these slow days
when tempo
creeps-
and
notes ring flat
'pon ivory key-
insistent
drums
of work-a-day clatter
bow humbly silent
in muted awe-
to velvet,
restful
sighs-
and
the soft,
simple joy-
of
pause.

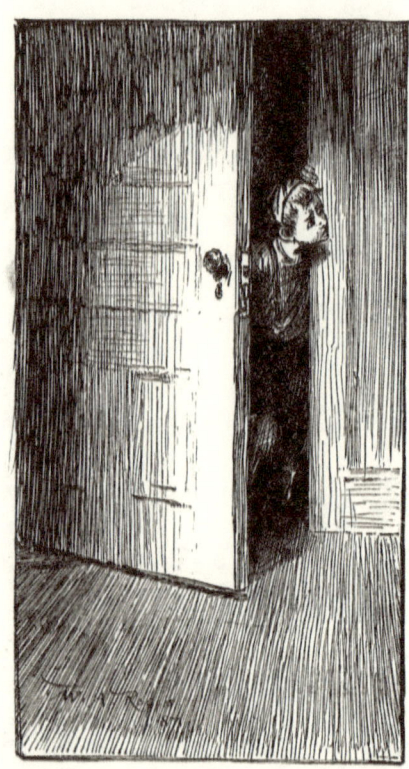

one door opens

one door opens-
one door closes
to the hallway
of stuckness
and pain-
a lace of
no color-
of gray and
sameness-
eternal sameness
with
no lighted
escape-
'cept to the
corridors
of
lonliness-
and
blackened window
stare.

one by one

one by one
bolts slide
latching the past-
sealing doors once open
silently-
closing out
all but scattered remnant
'bout hallway floor-
awaiting
the tumblers' click-
unlatching
the sun of
mysterious mornings.

old wood

old wood
old friends-
deep grain line'd
by time-
burnish'd
in sun's beam
and tempest-
polish'd
a'new
in dawning light-
of
two home's
warm glows.

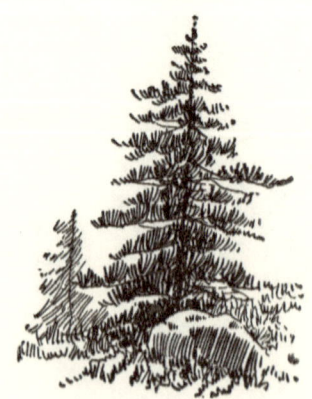

night

night
in the woods
holds all
in
inky black
embrace-
soundless
sleeping
of tree and critter-
save the whoo
of schreachy
owl
perched-
near shadowy branch'd fingers-
reaching
starward
to the
blackness.

oft times

⊘

oft times
the branches-
the clutter-
the noise-
of
life,
become as a veil-
obscuring,
hiding
the rainbow
moon
of gentle
pooled
light
beyond our grasp,
yet within
our hearts.

look
to
the light
at once outward-
yet inward
and see
the colors
of
meaning
in glorious
hue-
wrapped in
the velvet
of night
near
the edges
of truth.

for there
silently-
always silently
in seamless waiting
is-
the Way.

$\mathcal{B}$

travelers they be

❧

neither as dark
as blackened soot-
nor
perfect as white driven snow-
just travelers they be
one foot to next
in stumble-step tripped-
by small stone or word
midst the rainbow apparent-
both seen-
and feared.

yet-
deep in the hues of bottomless night-
and
stillness of new-breaking dawn-
souls as they
connected in rhythm-
sing to each other
in
mysterious cadence-
the joy of shared essence-
of bookended spirit
reserved for but few-
in the
lightening fast dash
of love
and-
of life.

B

morning

when morning breaks
and sun glints
slanting
through winter bare branch-
steel ice
yields
to glancing
rays-
stirring earthbound
things
in melting
gleem-
fueling frozen
life
with the
hope
of spring.

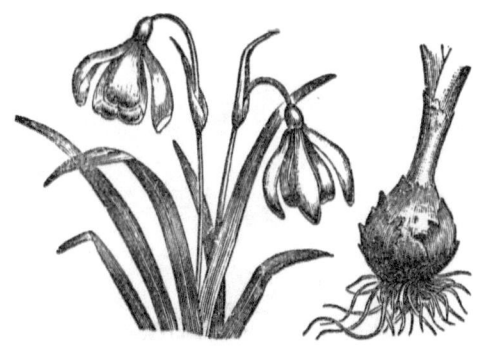

41

the wheel turns

୭

and so the wheel turns this day-
to
love in unexpected form
creeping silently upon us-
demanding us-
in the stillness
of november days
to reach outward-
embracing
that
which
once glimpsed-
must be
held
in dearness.

ß

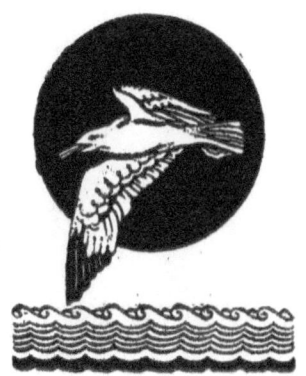

lost in thought

lost
in thought
ideas spring randomly
from the well
of
the Source
like unbidden
flighty birds
flapping
to some primordial
destination-
upward,
outward,
yet with
unknowing,
unerring flight-
to the places
of truth and
hope.

pearly moonlight

layered pearly moonlight
lying like shimmering pearl
'pon fall leaf-
as delicate colors reach
glowing
'tween
limb and branch.

'flected
night light
illumning
whitecaps below-
in a darting timless dance
of
natures' tune.

knots of life

℘

the knots of life
appear
unbidden-
tangled webs
of
rope
uyielding-
ever taut
with impatient tug.
yet
with simple
pull-
and
gentle hands-
knots unfold
in simple
march
like grain
before
approaching scythe-
one knot,
one tangle,
one stalk of
fielded
grain-
one life-
...at a time.

℘

wedding dress

❧

it is
after all-
airy and white
as new fallen snow
swirl'd to drifted brilliance-
layering
lightness
upon
lightness
in soundless swish-
floating gently
upon new life's
cusp,
'neath the sparkle
of radiant smile-
and the
assurance
of
dreams
fulfilled.

☙

it happens unbidden

it happens unbidden
this rush of words-
like a spigot wheel turned
in the instant of mind.

gurgling thought-
colored slants
of meaning and word-
crooked and
cascading up and out-
to be born
on page-
and-
there to live frozen
at the thinkers'
hand.

christmas day

it comes
midst frozen ground
and crystalline
pond
silently-
drawing each
to
windowed warmth
and glowing tree-
near
kin
and friend,
round
corners of time
now
burnished
by years-
shined
by smiles.
this treasured
jewel
called Christmas Day-
in bleak
december chill.

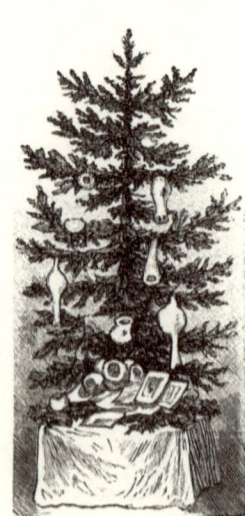

the underside of night

in the underside of night
down corridors of darkness-
steal glimmers and stirrings
like shadowed apparitions-
changing,
morphing-
and defying angular form.

they speak-
yet
hold silent counsel
and capture the resting soul
with seminal truths
too subtle
for daylight sun.

for in these darkened hallways of thought
the soul apprehends
truths of what is-
and discards
illusion
of daytime dreams
too grand.

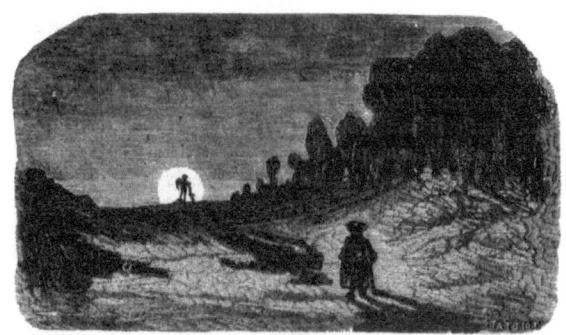

49

the song

her face is pretty too-
framed in song as it is-
the smile of creative passion long held
in the creases of her mind.

and so I listen to her song-
fine as its crafted-
and think of its harmony
matching my own.

enigma

her voice
screams no-

her murmurs
sigh yes-

'tween
poles of
fear
lie crystal truths-
sleeping
on beds
of gray
where
colorless gardens
grow
unnourished-
by the vita
of faith's
urging leap.

eye of light

❧

eye of light
gathering all thought
and being-
all knowing-
coloring life
broad stroked and bold,
subtly or softly,
gent'ly
painting what's real
in the creases of mind-
as it flows,
always flows-
from the
Source.

℔

snowy woods

ℰ

full moon'd
snowy woods
await-
with pearl cast
light
as from some
alchemists bowl-
bathing earthbound things
in shrouded
peace-
midst stone
and hilly knoll-
vague,
yet
certain
outlines of night-
caught with
glancing view-
revealing all Mystery
to
wondering
souls.

ℬ

gift of words

crusty with sleep
he arose
on the cusp of fall-
past a blaze-forced
summer interlude-
to find-neath the pines
the gift of words
kindly given
with caring thought-
to a traveler
on a twisty road
of renewal-
and
fire-temp'rd
discovery.

loft

framed by falling snow
'pon frozen ground-
lighted warmth
in winter chill
streams
lofted light-
to wooded
glen-
welcome beams
in winter's
chill.

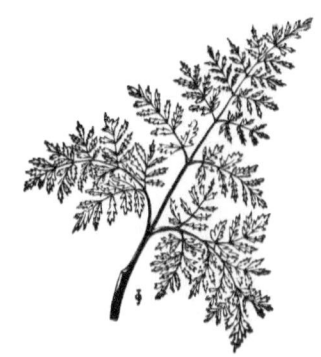

chill

ferbruary's
bitter chill'd air-
diamond faceted clear-
clean as scrubbed linen-
'pon snow humped
meadows-
cutting rapier like
into all
who venture forth
with crystal glance-
to behold
winter's
glory.

faceted ice

faceted ice
'pon
linen white
meadows-
traces
angled lines
of
february lesson-
crystal
brushed hue
in freeze shadowed
splendor,
while all creation-
sleeps.

consider these thoughts

consider these thoughts-
descending softly
as they must-
from sacred
bless'd places-
as light falling
snow
or goose down'd
feather-
growing slowly-
slowly-
with relentless
promise
in piled splendor
upon
untrodden ground
known to
but two-
'neath the sun
of a new-
dawning day.

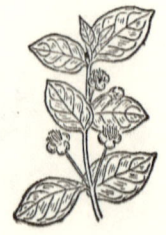

the sun rose

the sun rose
this day
o'r new fallen
snow mountains-
humped white linen
meadows
of ice.
the ruling orb
in triumph
smiling-
at winter gale
past
now vanquished-
by
feb- ruled
ray
and chased-
to
yesterdays
memory.
the orb
of life
asserting
his rightful
place-
insistent-
majestic-
'pon
the shoulder
of heaven.

joy

ॐ

christmas tree
and
snow'y
bough-

spark'ld glow
midst
frozen
night-

fire warmth
near
joyful
hearth-

children's smiles
'pon
breaking
day-

gathered warmth
of
kin
and friend-

music tone
in
glowing
space-

speak gentle peace-
on
Christmas Day.

note cards

colorful messages-
note cards
float-
with twisty turn
from tree-top to browning grass
'neath sunlit
azure sky-
telling the season turn
in cryptic verse
of timeless
rhyme.

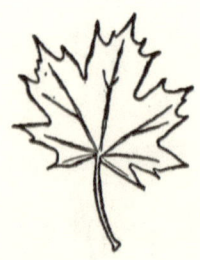

flowers and weeds

flowers and
weeds
both pretty in hue
side by side
in
gardens stand
radiant in noonday sun.

by turns they please
then find their way
to beauty and
perm'nence
in eye pleasing glow-
or
life choking transience
in mocking scorn.

choose your bloom
wisely
and be not deceived
for-
petals of spring color
deceptive in tone-
may strangle your
garden
with roots of
pain-
and petals
of hurt.

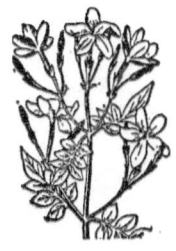

a world asleep

&

chimneys hunched clumsily
like smokey giants
'gainst white drift'd hills-
pencil lined plumes
floating lazily
toward
leaden sky-

trees long bare
like brown glazed chocolate-
stiff stick figures
in private bravery-
angling awkwardly
in tangled
disarray-

creeks rush noisily
like muff'ld drums
o'r frozen boulder gumdrops-
seeking the sea-
struggling downstream
tow'rd
final peace-

a world asleep-
suspended
in silent,
icy grip-
till april's
tears
touch waiting green shoots-
in the joyful
dance-
of spring.

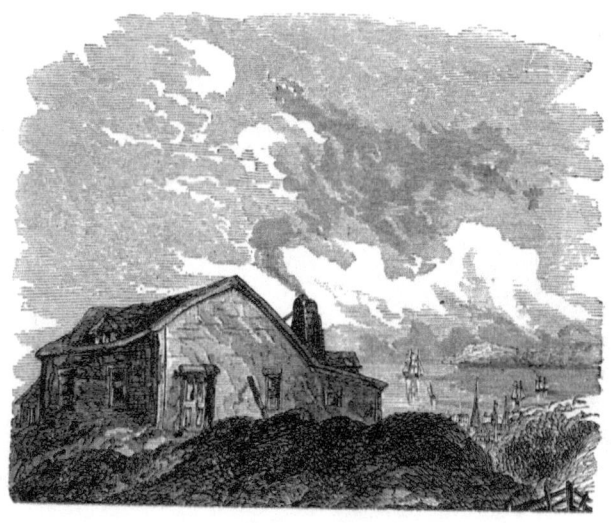

board by board

board by board it grew-
splinters rising
from an ice bound Januar'-
spring shoots
in a too soon season
rising upward,
ever upward
till space
and sky
soar in balance-
gathered sunlit
space
filled with hope-
and
rebirth.

life
from ashes-
possibility
from dream-
writ large
'pon
frozen ground.

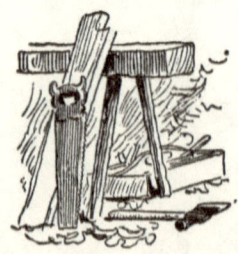

beyond knowing

something large beyond knowing
afoot and about-
everywhere and nowhere
ephemeral and ghostlike-
this pregnancy-
this expectant borning
of freshness and life
yet-
beyond
outreached grasp...
like fingers
it touches
all living places...
the demand of form--
yet unformed
this mystery.

the poet blinks
and sees not a thing-
but feels
this coming
in shadowed
wings
thru the lens
of night.

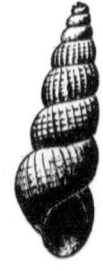

be still

be still-
for
in quiet lies
all healing,
all power,
all knowing,
all being,
beyond fragment
of thought
any mind
may hold.

be still-
for
in stillness
is heard
faintly-
yet with fortissimo crash,
all that is-
or ever can be-
in mysterious
octave of
breathless whisper.

be still.

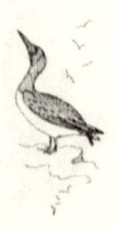

anticipation

awaiting
what comes-
what whispers round corners-
fills
soul and heart
with prism color joy
in
glorious hue-
touching
all things possible
in the
imminent offing-
for-
anticipation indeed
in all hearts joined-
bears in brilliance
the height
of
satisfaction.

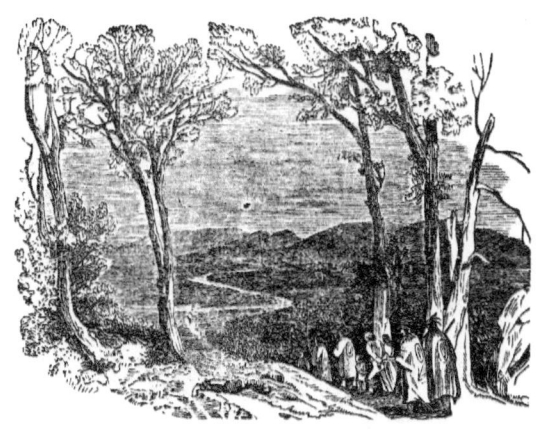

anger

crawling stealthily they are-
colors of anger
in kaleidoscope
prism-

mistrust and
intolearance-

envy and
greed-

jealousy and
rage-

impatience and
foreboding-

born as they are
of parent
fear-

creeping-
seeping-
insidious-
to mind
and
limb alike-

till-
paralysis and
dread
mark
once serene
paths-
down slippery walkways
of hate.

B

corridor of light

and so they laughed
those two-
giddy neath spring sun
and scented breeze-
silly with
improv'd stick
and
funny face look-
kids at play
in timeless fun,
thru a green
corridor of light-
seen by just two.

it grew

and so it grew in them
twin seeds planted
in distant soil-
stirrings
of
newer roots
silently sprouting-
relentless in gowth
and
yearning for the flower
that eternally
enfolds
the promise of
new life-
joined within
two
who water
and nourish
a sacred garden
of new beginnings-
midst the promise
of
shared,
unbounded
joy.

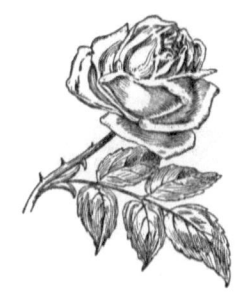

near clear water

words they drift upward
on cool morning breeze
near flower'd grove
and mossy tree-
born of quiet
to find
dancing life
under morning sun-
granting form to thought
as a gathering
white cloud
builds from nothingness-
to
perfect beauty.

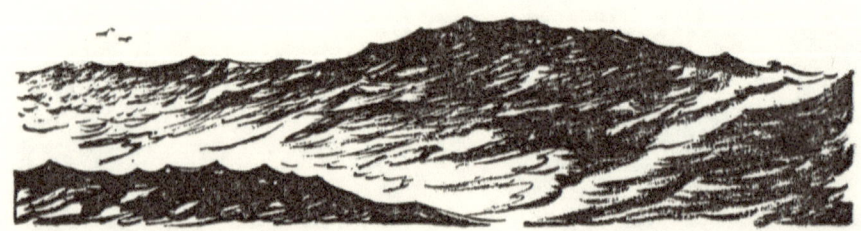

www.ingramcontent.com/pod-product-compliance
Lightning Source LLC
Chambersburg PA
CBHW022131170526
45157CB00004B/1830

* 9 7 8 1 4 6 5 3 8 7 1 3 4 *